Unleash the Resiliator Within

Resilience: A Handbook for Leaders

Also by Karen Ferris:
Game On! Change is Constant
Unleash the Resiliator Within—Resilience: A Handbook for Individuals

UNLEASH THE
RESILIATOR
WITHIN

RESILIENCE:
A HANDBOOK FOR LEADERS

KAREN FERRIS

Unleash the Resiliator Within
Resilience: A Handbook for Leaders

Copyright © Karen Ferris 2020

Typeset by BookPOD

ISBN: 978-0-6484694-2-1 (pbk) eISBN: 978-0-6484694-4-5

NATIONAL LIBRARY OF AUSTRALIA

A catalogue record for this book is available from the National Library of Australia

About the author

Karen Ferris is an unashamed organizational change management rebel with a cause. She likes to challenge the status quo but only when her reason for doing so is defensible.

Karen began her working life in IT but she has spent a large part of her career in the IT service management space where she is recognized globally for her expertise and insight.

As someone who is continually focused on the people side of change, Karen authored a publication titled *Balanced Diversity: A Portfolio Approach to Organizational Change* in 2010.

She considered herself an accidental author back then. She stumbled across a framework for embedding change, set out to write a white paper about it and ended up with a book. That was the moment she was propelled into the world of organizational change management.

In 2019, she published her second book *Game On! Change is Constant: Tactics to Win When Leading Change is Everyone's Business*. Karen is a sought after international keynote speaker, coach, mentor, facilitator and trainer.

Born in Liverpool, UK, she emigrated to Australia in 1998. She lives with her wife, Breed, in Melbourne. She is an avid Liverpool Football Club supporter, an Elvis fan, has an obsession with shoes, and is a self-confessed arctophile—you might want to Google that.

Contents

Introduction

Constant, volatile, uncertain, complex and ambiguous (VUCA) change is a reality. As competition and consumer demands increase, and as digital disruption intensifies, organizations and the individuals within them need to stop talking about resistance to change and start talking about resilience in the face of change.

We cannot control or manage change anymore. We must embrace the uncertainty and be ready to sense and respond, adapt and flex, diverge and converge, and be truly agile—all at a pace we've never experienced before.

In this environment, we need people at every level of an organization who can deal with the difficulties, demands, uncertainties and pressures of constant change without burning out. We need individuals who don't just bounce back from setbacks but who bounce forward and make good out of the situation. We need individuals who embrace change and are ready to adapt and reposition with confidence and self-reliance.

I have named these people, Resiliators. Resiliators thrives in the face of constant change; they possess a multitude of superpowers in order to do so.

This handbook is for anyone in an organization who leads others, and whose role, therefore, is to maintain and sustain resilience in others so they can say 'Game On!' in the face of constant change.

This handbook is also a companion to the *interactive Resiliator platform*, which is available to organizations in need of developing individual resilience across the entire workforce.

≈≈≈

The companion publication *Unleash the Resiliator Within—Resilience: A Handbook for Individuals* describes the superpowers of resilient individuals and the actions everyone can take to acquire them.

The Resiliator

What does the Resiliator look like?

In a nutshell, you are observing the Resiliator if you see the following traits:

Resiliators:

- Accept ambiguity and embrace uncertainty. They recognize and accept that they don't always have all the answers.
- Act thoughtfully. They assess a situation and respond to it rather than react to it. They are problem-solvers and carefully evaluate a situation before they try to resolve it.
- Manage their emotions. They have emotional intelligence.
- Are self-aware. They have a clear understanding of their strengths and weaknesses, thoughts and beliefs, motivations and emotions.
- Maintain a positive outlook with realistic optimism.
- Connect, collaborate and build networks.
- Operate with empathy. They are sensitive to the feelings of others and are able to demonstrate compassion and understanding.
- Maintain a growth mindset. They are accepting of failure as a means of learning and development.
- Are confident in their abilities and will make good use of their strengths while not focusing on their weaknesses.

Resilience

There are two sides to the resilience coin.

1. Equipping all individuals with the various superpowers they need to be resilient in the face of constant change.
2. Equipping those leading others with the knowledge and capability to maintain and sustain resilience in others.

This handbook deals with the latter. The companion handbook, *Unleash the Resiliator Within—Resilience: A Handbook for Individuals* deals with the former.

Remember, leadership is not about positions of authority or bestowed titles. Everyone can, and should, be a leader. Everyone, at all levels in the organization, can lead. In fact, in our world of constant and disruptive change, the organizations in which everyone leads will thrive.

Benefits for the individual

As an individual, there are numerous benefits to being resilient. These include:

*   Better physical and mental health.
*   Improved cognitive functioning.
*   Maintained inner calm in stressful situations.
*   Life perceived as a series of challenges not problems.
*   Stability in the face of a crisis.
*   Capacity to thrive in situations of high demand and ongoing pressure.
*   Ability to recover quickly from setbacks.
*   Failures and setbacks are seen as learning opportunities.
*   Reduced burnout.

- Increased sense of community.

How can you afford not to invest in yourself to become more resilient?

Benefits for the organization

Employees who are not resilient, soon become disengaged and either tune out or leave the organization.

According to Gallup's 2017 report *State of the Global Workplace,* 85% of adults worldwide are not engaged or are actively disengaged in the workplace.[1]

The report states that organizations in the top quartile of employee engagement, as opposed to those in the bottom quartile, realize benefits in the following areas:

- 17% higher productivity
- 21% higher profitability
- 59% lower turnover (in low-turnover organizations)
- 24% lower turnover (in high-turnover organizations)
- 41% lower absenteeism.

Gallup and other reports provide the cost of employee disengagement by country. These are some of the figures:

- Germany is 214.7 to 287.1 billion euros per year.[2]
- United States is 0.5 trillion dollars per year.[3]
- UK is 52–70 billion pounds per year.[4]

Return on investment

Spending money on building a resilient workforce returns dividends. Employee engagement increases and turnover decreases. Absenteeism and sick leave decrease, and productivity and motivation increase which leads to increased profitability.

In 2019, the World Health Organization published an information sheet titled *Mental Health in the Workplace*. It stated "Depression and anxiety have a significant economic impact; the estimated cost to the global economy is US$ 1 trillion per year in lost productivity."[5]

Back in 2014, PriceWaterhouseCoopers (PwC) undertook a return on investment analysis for Australian employers who wanted to create mentally healthy workplaces. To achieve that objective, PwC teamed up with Beyond Blue, the National Mental Health Commission, academic experts in mental health and the workplace, and further representatives from different workplace contexts.

The report *Creating a Mentally Healthy Workplace: Return on Investment Analysis* states that "through the successful implementation of an effective action to create a mentally healthy workplace, organisations, on average, can expect a positive return on investment (ROI) of 2.3."[6]

That is a return of 2.3 dollars for every dollar spent.

The World Health Organization also stated the ROI in mental health initiatives: "For every US$ 1 put into scaled up treatment for common mental disorders, there is a return of US$ 4 in improved health and productivity."[7]

Consequences

In 2019, the Victorian Government in Australia introduced workplace manslaughter laws.

The *Victorian Workplace Safety Legislation Amendment (Workplace Manslaughter and Other Matters) Act 2019* includes fines of up to 100,000 penalty units currently equating to AUD$16,522,000 for bodies corporate, and jail terms of up to 20 years for company officers who negligently cause a work-related death."[8]

So, if you are a 'company officer' who is found negligent in taking action to prevent mental health issues in the workplace that result in suicide, you could be facing up to two decades in jail and a hefty fine to boot.

There are other states in Australia with similar legislation.

In December 2019, three top corporate executives at French telecommunications company France Télécom (now Orange) were convicted of "collective moral harassment" and "institutional harassment" for creating a toxic work environment that led to 19 employee suicides and a further 12 employees who attempted to take their own lives. Former CEO, Didier Lombard, was sentenced to one year in jail, (of which 8 months were suspended), along with a €15,000 fine. His former deputy, Louis-Pierre Wenès, and human resources director, Olivier Barberot, received the same sentence and fine. Four other executives were given four-month suspended sentences and €5,000 fines.[9]

Can your organization afford *not* to take action?

Resilience and superpowers

It's all about the superpowers. In the face of constant change, we all need a range of superpowers at hand that will help us to be resilient. Only when the required superpower(s) are unleashed, can we thrive in the face of relentless and uncertain change.

Individual resilience is critical when the world around us is volatile, uncertain, complex and ambiguous. Resilience means we can adapt to difficult situations and not just survive but thrive. If we fail to adapt, the stress will overwhelm us, and we will suffer physically and mentally.

In addition to individual resilience, those tasked with leading people through constant change need additional superpowers to enable widespread resilience.

Here is my Resiliator model for leaders. It shows all the superpowers that leaders can utilize to create an environment for individual resilience and to build resilience in others.

> It is important to note that leaders should draw on both the superpowers for individuals and the superpowers for leaders.

Each superpower can be used at any time. Whichever you choose will depend on the context and situation you are facing. Multiple superpowers can be used at the same time, and the choice will be subject to the needs of the leader.

For example, a leader may observe that their team and the individuals within it are not sharing their thoughts and ideas. They do not speak up in meetings and appear reluctant to get involved in initiatives and improvements.

THE LEADER
DELEGATION AND TRUST

THE CONNECTOR
SHARED SENSE OF PURPOSE

THE REMOVALIST
REMOVE THE MENTAL HEALTH STIGMA

THE DIRECTOR
CLEAR DIRECTION

THE COMMUNICATOR
EFFECTIVE COMMUNICATION

THE REINFORCER
POSITIVE REINFORCEMENT

THE INCLUDER
TRUST AND INCLUSIVITY

THE REFLECTOR
REFLECTION AND RETROSPECTIVE

THE IDENTIFIER
IDENTIFY LOW RESILIENCE

THE MODELER
MODEL RESILIENCE

THE NURTURER
TRUST AND RESPECT

THE ENQUIRER
LEAD WITH QUESTIONS

THE AUTONOMIZER
EMPLOYEE AUTONOMY

THE DEVELOPER
CULTURE OF LEARNING

THE PROMOTER
PROMOTING SELF CARE

THE RESTRUCTURER
COGNITIVE RESTRUCTUING

THE CARETAKER
PSYCHOLOGICAL SAFETY

THE CULTIVATOR
ENVIRONMENT OF INNOVATION

THE ACCOUNTANT
PERSONAL ACCOUNTABILITY

THE PROTECTOR
LEAD WITH CARE AND COMPASSION

As a leader, your observations could suggest that you utilize the superpowers of the Caretaker and the Cultivator.

The Caretaker provides an environment of psychological safety. When psychological safety exists, people feel safe to speak their minds and contribute to discussions. They are prepared to take risks and stick their necks out knowing that they are safe to do so. There is mutual respect and there is no blame factor.

The Cultivator creates an environment for innovation and experimentation where successes and failures are celebrated. In this environment, there is also no blame factor. Everyone knows they can "have a go", and be curious, creative and collaborate. They are prepared to imagine, explore and come up with new ideas.

The combination of the Caretaker and the Cultivator superpowers means that people are prepared to have a go without fear of repercussion or ridicule. They know that there is no adverse consequence for trying something that didn't work the first time.

When people are comfortable with innovation and experimentation, they embrace failure as a learning opportunity.

Caution

It is important to note that you do not have to become an expert in utilizing all of the superpowers. You won't need all of them all of the time.

Each time you use a superpower, you will become better at it. Many of the superpowers need practice, so the more you use them, the better you become.

You will choose the superpower(s) you believe will best meet your needs in any given situation. Just like any other superhero, you will use the superpower(s) best suited to overcome the challenge currently in front of you. You can mix and match the superpowers as needed.

We will look at each of the Resiliator superpowers available to leaders.

Meet the Resiliators

Throughout this handbook, we will look at how the following group of Resiliators have used their superpowers.

Jason, Mayah, Sahar and Prayash are all in leadership roles at ABC Corporation. ABC Corporation is a large fashion retailer.

Jason has the longest tenure with the company. He has been with the organization for nine years and has had a leadership position in the property department for six years.

Mayah has been with the company for three years and has been a leader in the risk, audit and compliance department for all of that time.

Sahar is the newest leader. She has been with the organization for two years and in a leadership role for six months. She is a leader of a team in the call center.

Prayash is the leader of the marketing team and has been in that position with ABC Corporation for three years.

ABC Corporation has undergone considerable change as the retail industry is faced with increasing competition and technological disruption. The speed of change is not decreasing.

Jason, Mayah, Sahar and Prayash have all used the Resiliator superpowers to help navigate and lead through constant change.

We will hear from each of them, in their own words, as we look at each Resiliator superpower for leaders.

The Leader

Superpower: Leadership

Building, maintaining and sustaining a resilient workforce requires leaders, not managers.

Warren Bennis, one of the pioneers of contemporary leadership studies, is quoted as saying, "The manager does things right; the leader does the right thing."

No more command and control. Command and control and authoritarian direction has no place in the formation of resilient individuals. True leaders surrender control.

Leaders who "get out of the way" provide individuals with autonomy, delegate decision-making and allow them to experiment and take calculated and intelligent risks. If it fails, so be it, learn from it and move on.

Great leaders inspire and then get out of the way.

The superpowers, contained within the companion publication, which resilient individuals have include the Experimenter, the Adapter, the Explorer, the Collaborator and the Questioner. These superpowers will be stifled, if not exterminated, in a command and control environment.

A leader who controls everything and has no tolerance for risk taking demotivates employees and stifles innovation and experimentation. Controlling leaders—who are managers not leaders—create bottlenecks rather than increase throughput. They signal a lack of trust and confidence.

The manager relies on control. The leader inspires trust. There is an argument that leaders both lead and manage. They generate innovation, creativity and experimentation as leaders and then they execute as managers. However, the crux is that the leadership qualities and capabilities will establish and preserve resilience.

Guardrails

Many people believe that if they let go of control and "get out of the way", there will be anarchy. This is not the case.

Leaders provide individuals with guardrails or principles by which they operate. Guardrails on the road stop drivers from ending up in dangerous areas. They are placed in the most problematic areas, where it is easy to do the wrong thing.

Although we can give everyone the autonomy to self-manage and make decisions, sometimes, individuals need guardrails to make sure their efforts are aligned with the organizational needs. This also gives them comfort and confidence to step out of their comfort zone and have a go.

Guardrails should be agreed upon. They are arbitrary rules to guide employees. Leaders could select a representative cross-functional group of employees to define the guardrails and then put them up for comment from the rest of the organization.

Once as-near-as-possible consensus has been achieved, they should be published and subject to regular review based on ongoing feedback.

In addition to organization-wide guardrails, teams may have additional guardrails specific to their function and the work they carry out.

Guardrails are the guidelines within which employees can act autonomously. They enable employees to make good decisions. Unlike rules, which are constrictive, guardrails allow employees to use their intuition, rational thinking and their unique contextual understanding of the situation. Focus on the guardrails (principles) not policies.

HR technology company, Paycor, has six guardrails or guiding principles listed on its website. They are shown below.[10]

Take care of customers first	Our customers are our heroes. When they win, we win.
Do the right thing	Because it always works out in the long run.
Take care of each other	There's nothing better than working with friends who look out for you.
Think big, dream big	Never say never! Solve problems, invent a better way, and disrupt the status quo.
Compete to win	We embody the spirit of success in everything we do: in our habits, routines, relationships and in the energy and accountability we bring to the game.
Have fun along the way	Buckle up, it's a fast-paced business. That's why we celebrate the wins, laugh in the face of adversity and enjoy the ride.

Clarity

The Leader provides clarity of purpose. When leaders are clear about what needs to be achieved and why, everyone is on the same page. Everyone is working toward the same goal.

If leaders are not clear, then teams will become confused, lose their sense of direction, and become distracted and unproductive when directions shift, plans change and teams grow.

This results in chaos. Leadership is about keeping teams away from chaos and moving toward a place of clarity. Chaos results in unmotivated and disengaged individuals with low resilience.

Clarity and a shared sense of purpose is motivational and engages individuals in achievement of a common goal.

At Google, there is one goal. It is clearly stated on their website.[11]

"Our mission is to organize the world's information and make it universally accessible and useful."

Everyone at Google works toward the same goal. They can do it how they like but there is a common destination or purpose.

In their words

Jason's story

When I became the leader of the property department, I wanted to know how the department was performing. I arranged to speak to a range of my stakeholders, and over the first two to three weeks, I made numerous telephone calls.

Overall, feedback was positive but there was one negative observation that kept arising. It was the excessive time it took to get property repairs done in the stores. This intrigued me because each geographical area we covered had a local property manager.

I convened a meeting of all the local property managers and asked for their insights. The problem was immediately clear. The local property managers did not have any autonomy in regard to spend. When a local repair was required, they had to contact head office and get authorization before they could proceed with the required works. My predecessor had insisted on signing off on absolutely everything.

I instructed the local property managers that they no longer had to get authorization to carry out repairs and had the autonomy to make informed decisions and get the work done. We co-designed some principles or guardrails to help them in the decision-making process.

Principles included not purchasing anything that would introduce risk to employees, customers, the store or the organization; and equipment had to comply with the relevant country standard.

Stakeholders reported immediate improvement with repair time reductions of up to 85%. All I had to do was get out of the way.

Actions

Create an environment of delegation and trust and allow individuals to utilize their superpowers unhindered.

Create guardrails. Initially, they can be simple (like the ones listed below) and can be developed and refined later.

- Do the right thing by the customer.
- Do the right thing by your colleagues.
- Do the right thing by the company.

Provide clarity of purpose. Start with why. It should be inspiring and should change something for the better. It should serve the greater good.

Have a plan and a shared destination.

Have clear responsibilities for everyone.

Maintain the clarity. Check-in often and reiterate the purpose.

📖 Reading

Freedom from Command and Control: Rethinking Management for Lean Service by John Seddon

The New One Minute Manager by Ken Blanchard and Spencer Johnson

Leaders Eat Last: Why Some Teams Pull Together and Others Don't by Simon Sinek

Measure What Matters: How Google, Bono, and the Gates Foundation Rock the World with OKRs by John Doerr

A Sense of Purpose: Discovering Your Personal Mission Statement by Stephen R. Covey

🌐 Links

TED Talk: Why the secret to success is setting the right goals by John Doerr
https://www.ted.com/talks/john_doerr_why_the_secret_to_success_is_setting_the_right_goals

TED Talk: How great leaders inspire action by Simon Sinek
https://www.ted.com/talks/simon_sinek_how_great_leaders_inspire_action

The Communicator

Superpower: Communication

The Communicator has excellent communication skills. Effective communication builds positive relationships that promote resilience at work.

The Communicator keeps everyone informed about what is happening. When people feel engaged and involved with what is happening around them, they are far more resilient than they would be if they felt they were being kept in the dark.

There are enough sources of information around communication to warrant a book in itself but I am going to highlight what I believe to be the most important considerations and techniques in order to get communication right.

Effective communication

Clarity

The communication and its message should be easily understood. The Communicator delivers a message with clarity. There is no room for ambiguity. If a message is not clear, people will fill in the perceived gaps with their own interpretation. Messages not only become corrupted but also become the new but flawed reality.

Validation

Effective communication takes place when a person sends a message and it is received and understood as intended by the recipients.

The Communicator checks to determine if the message has been understood as it were intended.

They ask questions of the recipients to determine what has been heard. If the message has not been interpreted correctly, they correct their communication.

Listen

Often, we communicate to respond. First, we should communicate to listen, then we respond.

The Communicator listens to the questions people are asking and ensures that future communication addresses these questions.

Two-way channel

Communication is not about sending out a blanket email. That is a broadcast.

Effective communication takes place when recipients are provided with a channel to ask questions and seek clarification.

This could be via a collaboration platform.

Share

When people are asking questions, there are likely to be many others with the same question who are not prepared to speak up.

Capture questions asked and turn them into Frequently Asked Questions (FAQs) that everyone can access easily.

Medium

The Communicator gives careful consideration to the medium used for communication. Communication could be verbal or written and could be delivered physically or digitally. The medium will depend on the preference of the receiver(s).

Mediums include face-to-face, over the phone, video conference, email, and text and social media.

Frequency

There is also careful consideration of the frequency of communication of a particular message required by the receiver. Agree with the various stakeholders, the frequency at which they would like to receive communication. Remember, there is no such thing as over-communication.

Timing

In addition to frequency, timing is important. Consider the best time for the recipients to read and digest the communication.

For example, it's probably not an optimum time to run a town hall meeting on a Friday afternoon when most employees are thinking about the weekend. Sending an email first thing on a Monday morning is not an optimum time as it can get lost in the already busy inboxes filled with weekend mail.

Push or pull?

Communication can be delivered through push or pull methods or both. Again, this should be determined by the needs of the intended audience.

Push methods are where the message is pushed out to the audience; whereas, pull methods are where the audience retrieves the message when they want it. Push methods include email, letter, desk drop, presentations etc.

Pull methods include information hosted on an intranet, a knowledge base or collaboration platform that people can access when and if they wish.

Storytelling

Storytelling is a highly effective communication method. Stories are illustrative, easily memorable and allow the communicator to create stronger emotional bonds with the recipients.

When we hear stories, we are more engaged than we would be by just hearing about data and facts. When we read or hear data alone, the language part of the brain works to understand it.

When we read or hear a story, not only does the language part of the brain start to work, but other parts of the brain we would use if we were actually experiencing what we are reading or hearing, start working too.

It is far easier to remember stories than data or facts.

Pictures

It is not a cliché when we say, "a picture paints a thousand words". It is true. For example, which of these is easier to understand?

A circle is a simple closed shape. It is the set of all points in plane that create a given distance from a given point, the center; equivalently it is the curve traced out by a point that moves so that its distance from a given point is constant.

oR

circle

If you can use images and graphics to enhance your message, do so.

Pervasive

Communications have to be pervasive. They have to spread throughout the organization. Cisco's white paper titled *Transitioning to Workforce 2020* states:

> To establish a powerful, viable culture, leaders will first have to build a collaborative infrastructure facilitated by pervasive communications. Everyone must be able to communicate with everyone, wherever they are, whenever necessary. The organization must have the means to bring individuals together constantly, not only to convey information but also to mutually share that information across the whole range of workgroups that continually materialize and dissolve in response to business requirements.[12]

In their words

Sahar's story

My team members in the call center were pretty good customer service representatives when I became their leader six months ago. As a new leader, I wanted to improve on that and build the best-rated customer service team in the call center.

I had heard that storytelling was a powerful communication tool, so I decided to try it out. I told a story about my previous position in a call center at a large shoe retailer. The company culture was one of fanatical customer service. Just like ABC Corporation, we were not judged on how long we spent on the phone but rather on happy customers.

I told the story about how one day, a lonely woman called the call center and asked lots of questions. This turned into a conversation. Hours later, the customer and I decided to take a break. Then, not too long later, she called again and our conversation continued. Most of the conversation had nothing to do with shoes but it had everything to do with customer happiness. The phone call lasted a total of 6 hours, which was a record at the time. It was not too long after that that record was broken by an 8-hour conversation.

After telling that story, my team was clearly enthused and motivated. They had engaged with my story. Our team became the best-rated customer service team the following month. We continued to be rated in the top 5 as we continued with our storytelling. Our objective was not to have long calls with customers but to provide excellent customer service. These exceptions just highlighted what we would do to achieve that objective.

Actions

Before delivering communication (verbal or non-verbal), get someone else to read it or listen to it, and ensure it is clear and without ambiguity.

Perform an A/B test when communicating to a wide audience. Use a medium, for example, email, where you want the recipients to take a particular course of action such as clicking on a link to access further information. Create two versions of the communication: A and B.

Version A will have one variable different to Version B. It could be that A contains a graphic and B does not.

For example, create two versions of an email in which you want the recipients to click on a link. Send version A to a sample group of 30 people, or thereabouts, and send version B to another sample group of the same number. Determine whether communication A or B worked best based on how many people clicked on the link. Use the best performing communication to go to the wider audience.

Validate that your communication is being understood by asking the recipient(s) questions regarding the message you wished them to receive. For example: What did they hear? What was the key message?

Hone your listening skills. Provide channels for people to ask questions, seek clarification, discuss and enable dialogue to take place. Look at collaboration platforms that may already be in use within your organization, and leverage them. Utilize other methods such as question boards and Lean Coffee sessions.

Collect frequently asked questions and publish them. Make them easily accessible.

Continually seek feedback on the effectiveness of your communication, including content, medium, frequency, timing etc.

Use graphics and metaphors where possible, and utilize the power of storytelling.

Reading

Crucial Conversations: Tools for Talking When Stakes Are High by Kerry Patterson, Joseph Grenny, Ron McMillan and Al Switzler

How to Win Friends and Influence People by Dale Carnegie

Stories for Work: The Essential Guide to Business Storytelling by Gabrielle Dolan

Links

Lean Coffee
http://agilecoffee.com/leancoffee/

Storytelling
https://www.khanacademy.org/partner-content/pixar/storytelling

https://www.ted.com/talks/andrew_stanton_the_clues_to_a_great_story?utm_campaign=tedspread&utm_medium=referral&utm_source=tedcomshare

The Identifier

Superpower: Identification

Signs

The Identifier identifies the signs of low resilience early and takes immediate action. When an individual shows signs of low resilience, it is often a mental health issue. It could be the result of stress, anxiety, fatigue or other factors.

The Identifier constantly looks for signs of low resilience so that action can be taken before the situation worsens.

The Identifier looks for the following:

Change in behavior. When a person's behavior is different to their normal behavior. This could be increased irritability, agitation or cynicism.

Motivation. When a person suddenly lacks motivation for their job, whereas, they previously had a sense of purpose and drive.

Increased mistakes or lapses in judgment. When a person, whom you know is competent and good at their job, starts making errors or poor choices.

Focus. When a person demonstrates reduced concentration and is having trouble focusing.

Problem solving. When a person is becoming overwhelmed by simple problems.

Sick leave. When increased sick leave is being taken and when higher rates of minor illnesses are increasing. When low resilience occurs, it's not uncommon to see a corresponding rise in absenteeism and sick days.

Tiredness, weariness or sleepiness. The signs include dropping heads, incessant yawning and eyelids that seem to be closing.

Interoffice conflict. When there is lack of collaboration or simmering feuds between employees or decreased interaction in meetings and continued unresolved conflict.

Planning. When there is a lack of planning for the future. Demonstrated behavior when responding to daily issues is more reactive than proactive. There is no anticipation of issues and opportunities.

Productivity. When there is a decrease in productivity for no apparent reason.

Morale. When there is decreased morale, employees look down and disengaged.

Language. When there is use of defeatist language such as "I can't" or "It won't work."

Leaders have to recognize that they don't have to have the answers to a person's low resilience. The cause may be something over which they have no control. They have to recognize that they are not medical practitioners, psychologists or psychiatrists.

The Identifier, having identified low resilience, reaches out to the person and asks "Are you ok?"

R U OK? is an Australian non-profit suicide prevention organization, founded by advertiser Gavin Larkin in 2009. It revolves around the slogan "R U OK?", and it advocates for people to have meaningful conversations with others that could save lives.

The R U OK? website (link in the Links section below) has amazing resources—many available to download—that can assist in (a) identification of low resilience and (b) knowing what to do. The following four steps are from the website.[13]

1. Ask R U OK?

- Be relaxed, friendly and concerned in your approach.
- Help them open up by asking questions like "How are you going?" or "What's been happening?"
- Mention specific things that have made you concerned for them, like "You seem less chatty than usual. How are you going?"
- If they don't want to talk, don't criticize them.
- Tell them you're still concerned about changes in their behavior and you care about them.
- Avoid a confrontation.
- You could say "Please call me if you ever want to chat" or "Is there someone else you'd rather talk to?"

2. Listen with an open mind

- Take what they say seriously, and don't interrupt or rush the conversation.

- Don't judge their experiences or reactions but acknowledge that things seem tough for them.

- If they need time to think, sit patiently with the silence.

- Encourage them to explain by asking "How are you feeling about that?" or "How long have you felt this way?"

- Show that you've listened by repeating back what you've heard (in your own words) and ask if you have understood them properly.

3. Encourage action

- Ask "What have you done in the past to manage similar situations?"

- Ask "How would you like me to support you?"

- Ask "What's something you can do for yourself right now? Something that's enjoyable or relaxing?"

- You could say, "When I was going through a difficult time, I tried this... You might find it useful too."

- If they've been feeling really down for more than two weeks, encourage them to see a health professional. You could say, "It might be useful to link in with someone who can support you. I'm happy to assist you to find the right person to talk to."

- Be positive about the role of professionals in getting through tough times.

4. Check in

- Pop a reminder in your diary to call them in a couple of weeks. If they're really struggling, follow up with them sooner.

- You could say, "I've been thinking of you and wanted to know how you've been going since we last chatted."

- Ask if they've found a better way to manage the situation. If they haven't done anything, don't judge them. They might just need someone to listen to them for the moment.

- Stay in touch and be there for them. Genuine care and concern can make a real difference.

The conversation may also inform the Identifier of actions they can take to prevent low resilience in the workplace.

In their words

Sahar's story

I noticed that Jim's productivity had fallen. He was resolving fewer customer issues than in previous weeks and some of the advice he was giving customers was not the best advice he could have given.

I watched Jim's behavior for a little while to determine if it were a blip or something more concerning. His behavior was clearly different to his normal behavior, and he looked tired and weary.

During a shift break, when no one else was around, I spoke to Jim. I said, "Jim. I have noticed a change in your behavior recently. You seem to be distracted. Are you ok?"

Knowing Jim was a very proud person and of a generation that didn't talk about anxiety, fatigue or mental health, I wasn't sure I would get any response other than, "Yes of course I am."

My assumption was wrong. Jim welcomed someone reaching out to him. It was clear that Jim wanted to talk so we went to a quiet room and I listened.

His five-year-old niece had been killed in a car accident four weeks ago and Jim was traumatized. He was trying to support his brother while coming to terms with the loss himself. He wasn't sleeping and was finding it difficult to do his job. His resilience was at its lowest. He was extremely depressed.

After letting Jim talk, I suggested we contact the Employee Assistance Program as they provide confidential counseling. We made the call and Jim had a counseling session that same afternoon.

I checked in with Jim on a regular basis to find out how he was feeling and if the counseling was helping. It turned out it was what Jim needed and he confided in me some weeks later that if I hadn't reached out, he felt he may have shifted from depressed to suicidal.

I am glad I asked, "Are you ok?"

Actions

Keep your eyes and ears open for signs of low resilience.

Use the R U OK? four steps.

Visit the R U OK? website for resources.

DO the following:[14]

- Reassure the person that you are genuinely concerned about them and that they can talk to you when they need to.
- Be understanding and patient but also be encouraging and confident.
- Help the person to talk about the specific issues and problems they are experiencing rather than generalized 'complaining'.
- Assist the person in developing an action plan. Later, follow up and check how they are going.
- Encourage them to access appropriate support and, if appropriate, professional treatment.
- Provide specific, honest, timely and development-orientated feedback.

DON'T do the following:

- Don't tell the person, "we all get stressed" and to "snap out of it."
- Don't tell the person to (a) not think about it (b) that it will all get better soon (c) that there is nothing to worry about (d) that it's not that bad or (e) that they shouldn't show weakness in the workplace.
- Don't ignore the problem when you talk to the person or avoid talking to them about important issues.
- Don't make assumptions.

Reading

Managing for Resilience: A Practical Guide for Employee Wellbeing and Organizational Performance by Monique F. Crane

Links

R U OK? https://www.ruok.org.au/

The Autonomizer

Superpower: Autonomy

The Autonomizer provides employees with autonomy: the freedom to do their job their way.

Autonomy gives employees the power to shape their work environment in ways that allow them to perform at their best.

The benefit to both the employee and the organization is that employees are happier, more engaged, more committed and motivated, more productive and less likely to leave the organization.

Autonomy does not mean anarchy. The Autonomizer provides employees with guardrails and clarity of purpose as discussed in The Leader superpower.

Although freedom of choice is key to autonomy, too much choice is dangerous. Guardrails are boundaries and a system to hold people accountable for their results. This allows autonomy to flourish. Within clear boundaries, people are empowered to determine how they will achieve their goals.

Clarity means that the Autonomizer has provided clear and unambiguous direction for their employees. The goals, outcomes, and expectations are absolute.

In addition to provision of guardrails and clarity, the following need to be taken into account to provide autonomy.

Start small

For many leaders, providing autonomy is moving from an environment of command and control to one of delegation and trust. This can be a huge shift in mindset and ways of working.

However, leaders do not have to do this in one massive leap. They can take small steps.

Find a small, low-risk initiative and assign the task to a team member. Explain that you are trying to change your leadership style to provide more employee freedom.

Be clear about the task at hand, your expectations, required outcomes and completion date. Agree on the check-in frequency.

Let your employee know that you are there to support and remove obstacles as needed, and that they can reach out at any time in-between the scheduled check-ins.

At the check-ins, confirm that the frequency of check-ins is working and if it isn't, amend the frequency. As a leader, you provide feedback to the employee and vice versa. This is most likely a learning experience for both of you.

At the end of this exercise, you will have a more engaged employee and more time available for yourself.

Rinse and repeat. Now provide other employee(s) with a task and the autonomy to complete it as they wish.

Consistency

Some leaders provide autonomy only to rein in control when a crisis occurs.

Provision of autonomy must be consistent. Instead of reining in control as soon as a crisis is perceived, you should create a renewed focus of utilizing the strengths of the people around you.

Gather the team and determine how best to deal with the crisis. Inconsistency is heard as "I trust you to do the right thing but only when it is smooth sailing. I don't trust you when the going gets tough." This leads to mistrust, doubt, confusion and disengagement.

Trust

If you want to provide autonomy, you have to trust your employees to do the right thing. When this happens, employees feel they are an integral part of the team.

When employees have a leader who trusts them, they are more engaged and productive. You need to trust your employees and let them get on with the job within the guardrails provided. You must not then undermine this trust later by taking back control. You need to be consistent.

You have to demonstrate trust. You have to be self-aware in order to recognize when your actions may demonstrate a lack of trust. Trusting an employee doesn't mean they know you trust them. Trust can be demonstrated by not admonishing an employee when something does not go as planned. Trust means tolerating mistakes and using them as opportunities to learn.

Transparency

To provide autonomy, you need to be transparent. You need to share information and be open and honest. Doing so tells employees that you trust them with the truth. People often intuitively know when information is being kept from them, which translates to "you don't trust me."

With transparency comes trust and respect.

Being honest is perhaps one of the most difficult ideas for many leaders. When leaders learn to be transparent, for example to tell the truth, they have to trust their employees with that truth. This can be a big leap of faith. If leaders are truly transparent, they are telling employees that they trust them with the truth, even in the most difficult circumstances.

Transparency also means you share your own mistakes and challenges with your employees. Transparency equals integrity, honesty, vulnerability, humility and trust.

Embrace mistakes

Mistakes will be made. Do not be destructively critical when mistakes are made. This will kill initiative and, consequently, employee engagement.

Innovation and creativity do not happen when people work in fear. See mistakes as learning experiences. With each mistake, you are moving nearer to success.

Celebrate the mistakes and the successes.

Capability

Make sure your employee has the capability and competency to undertake the task you are giving them. Ensure they have the necessary tools and resources available. Do everything you can to set them up for success.

In their words

Mayah's story

As a leader in the risk, audit and compliance department, I guess I was inherently risk adverse. I was increasingly micromanaging my staff, especially in my early days as a leader. I wanted to be in control.

What was noticeable was the disengagement of staff and the lack of motivation.

After a number of conversations with my team and my peers, the cause was clear. My staff had no autonomy. There was no freedom to undertake tasks in their way. It was my way or the highway!

I sought out a leadership coach who helped me move from a command and control way of leading to one of delegation and trust.

It was accomplished in small steps. I provided my team with guardrails that included an assessment of risk. I told my team that if we were shooting above the water line, we could probably fix the damage. However, if we were shooting below the water line, we probably couldn't fix the damage and we would sink. This allowed the team to assess risk without me being overly prescriptive. I had to trust my team to do the right thing and my team had to see that trust consistently.

Magic happened as I gave up more control and just got out of the way. Motivation, engagement and productivity increased. I had more time to focus on the things I should always have been focusing on.

Actions

There are some key rules around provision of autonomy. Make sure you action these.

1. Clarity: Be absolutely clear of the outcomes you are looking for. Be clear about timeframe, budget and frequency of communication, for example, progress updates.

2. Hear it back: Ask your employees to confirm their understanding of what is required to ensure there is common understanding. This is critical for successful delegation and, if not carried out, can result in disaster for all parties. The employee might think they are 100% clear about what you require and work relentlessly to achieve the outcome, only to find out that what they are working on is not what you wanted at all. It is devastating for both you and your employee and has an adverse impact on morale.

3. Ensure capability: Ensure your employee has the required skills and capabilities to undertake the job at hand. Don't make assumptions. There may be some level of training or guidance needed.

4. Open channels: Ensure there are open channels for you to obtain updates on progress and for your employee to ask for clarification or guidance. Be careful not to repeatedly ask for updates. Provision of autonomy means you trust your employee to get on with the job and provide you with updates as per the agreed communication frequency.

5. Feedback: Provide positive feedback and reinforcement for the employee. Encourage your employee to provide you with feedback.

6. Lessons learnt: You and your employee should conduct a 'lessons learnt' session. What did you, as the leader, learn? What did the employee learn? What actions are you both going to take to improve next time?

📖 Reading

Drive: The Surprising Truth About What Motivates Us by Daniel H. Pink

Emergent: Ignite Purpose, Transform Culture, Make Change Stick by Stephen Scott Johnson

🌐 Links

I, Tomato: Morning Star's radical approach to management
https://www.youtube.com/watch?v=qqUBdX1d3ok

The Caretaker

Superpower: Psychological safety

The Caretaker makes sure there is psychological safety in the workplace.

The term "psychological safety" was first coined by Amy C. Edmondson in her 1999 research study of workplace teams. Edmondson is a Harvard Business School professor and defines psychological safety as "a belief that one will not be punished or humiliated for speaking up with ideas, questions, concerns or mistakes."

Her research in the 1990s, across numerous US hospitals, sought to find out if better teams make fewer mistakes. What she discovered was just the opposite of what she had expected: it was the most cohesive hospital teams that were seemingly making the most mistakes—not fewer.

Further investigation revealed that the better teams weren't making more mistakes but that they were more able and willing to talk about their mistakes.

This became Edmondson's influential 1999 paper, titled *Psychological Safety and Learning Behavior in Work Teams.*

Since then, her research has continued to show that psychological safety can make teams *and* entire organizations perform better.

In 2015, Google published the results of Project Aristotle, a two-year study into what makes a great team. The interesting thing was that the answer wasn't *those with the most senior people, with the highest IQs or even those who made the least number of mistakes.* Google found five key dynamics that made great teams successful, and the leading dynamic was psychological safety.

The Google *re:Work* guide on team effectiveness describes psychological safety as:

> Psychological safety refers to an individual's perception of the consequences of taking an interpersonal risk or a belief that a team is safe for risk taking in the face of being seen as ignorant, incompetent, negative, or disruptive. In a team with high psychological safety, teammates feel safe to take risks around their team members. They feel confident that no one on the team will embarrass or punish anyone else for admitting a mistake, asking a question, or offering a new idea.[15]

When team members sense psychological safety, they will speak out, share ideas, take risks, and be innovative and creative. They do this knowing they will not be ridiculed in the process. They know that their contribution to a discussion is a valued one.

They feel able to speak up, question and challenge, and present new thoughts and ideas without adverse repercussion.

This is what is needed if organizations are to be creative, and are able to experiment and innovate to stay ahead of the competition. It is what is needed for employees to be resilient in the face of constant change. They can speak openly, ask questions, ask for support, challenge the status quo, challenge ideas and initiatives, and present better ways of doing things.

How do you create an environment of psychological safety?

Lead by example

You need to set an example for employees. This means asking for upward feedback, acknowledging your mistakes, being open to opinions that are different to yours, being available and approachable, and encouraging people to ask questions and challenge assumptions.

If you don't admit your mistakes, no one, in a room where they consider everyone to be perfect, is going to speak up. When you admit you have made a mistake, you are encouraging others to do the same.

Courage

Be vulnerable. Admit if you don't know something and ask others for their input. Share your feelings; tell your team when you feel frustrated or stressed, motivated or inspired. When you do this, others will do the same.

Replace criticism with curiosity

If something has not gone according to plan, don't assume you know the reason why. Do not criticize your employees. Instead explore what went wrong with curiosity.

Focus on the resolution rather than the fault.

Active listening

Active listening means that employees feel valued, have a sense of belonging and are contributing to the team.

Active listening means being present, *really* hearing what people are saying, validating your understanding by repeating what was said, encouraging people to share more by asking them questions, and encouraging those not participating to speak up and be involved.

Safety

As a leader, you need to create the safety. This means you need to exhibit these behaviors and guide your team to do the same. When these behaviors are not exhibited, they need to be called out and challenged.

- Do not interrupt when someone is speaking.
- Keep an open mind.
- There is no judgment.
- All ideas are accepted.
- There is no blame.
- There is no bad idea, however wacky.
- The crazier, the better.

Structure

You may put in place systems and structures by having some "rules" around meetings and behaviors.

This could be a meeting charter that lists expected behaviors such as the ones listed in the previous "safety" section.

Inclusiveness

Include team members in decision-making. Gather their feedback and opinions and value each and every contribution. Explain how you came to make particular decisions and acknowledge the input of others. Invite the team to challenge your ideas.

Healthy conflict

If conflict arises, approach it as a mediator and ask, "How can we achieve a mutual desirable outcome?"

Try an exercise called "Just like me." This helps people put themselves in someone else's position and helps resolve conflict. It promotes empathy. The exercise gets participants to reflect and consider perspectives like:

- This person has beliefs, perspectives and opinions just like me.
- This person has hopes, anxieties and vulnerabilities just like me.
- This person has friends, family and perhaps children who love them just like me.
- This person wants to feel respected, appreciated and competent just like me.
- This person wishes for peace, joy and happiness just like me.

Difficult conversations

Leaders should try and anticipate reactions and plan responses when difficult conversations are likely to arise. Leaders can be prepared and confront the situation head-on. Gather concrete evidence to support a position. Anticipate the questions or arguments that may arise. Think about the possible objections or arguments and what your response will be. Look for any weaknesses in your position and mitigate them.

Trust

Leaders have to establish and keep trust. There will be no psychological safety without it.

Trust is established when you hold yourself accountable and do what you said you would do. This helps people to see you as competent and dependable.

The team has to see its leader as its ally. Treat your team with compassion and respect. Practice empathy. Don't judge your team when things go wrong. Work with your team to learn from the opportunity the failure presents. Leaders need emotional intelligence.

Measure

Amy C. Edmondson created a Psychological Safety Assessment.

You can access it here:
https://www.comparativeagility.com/capabilities/psychological-safety-assessment/

Create your own version, based on the one above, to measure the level of psychological safety within your team.

Use simple statements that require a Yes or No answer such as the following:

- When someone makes a mistake in this team, it is often held against them.
- In this team, it is hard to discuss difficult issues and problems.
- In this team, people are sometimes rejected for being different
- It is not completely safe to take a risk in this team.
- It is difficult to ask other members of this team for help.

In their words

Prayash's story

I guess most people want to look good and have others think well of them at work, but that means if they don't feel safe, they'll hold back saying things others may not like.

I realized the need for psychological safety having read Amy C. Edmondson's book The Fearless Organization.

I realized that my team was reticent, backward in coming forward, and had poor contributions due to a lack of psychological safety. This was an organizational cultural issue, but I was determined to change that through the Caretaker superpower. I hoped that the outcome would spread through osmosis.

As a team, we set some ground rules for our behaviors that would make each other feel safe to contribute. We held each other accountable for those agreed behaviors and we felt safe to call them out when they weren't followed—as we had agreed upon.

I made sure that I was transparent and authentic, that I acknowledged my mistakes and that I talked about my weaknesses and areas for improvement as an individual and leader.

The team became more innovative and creative. Two years ago, we won an AME Award for our ground-breaking thinking in the marketing space.

✎ Actions

Create a psychological safety assessment survey as a baseline.

Create a plan of action to improve the psychological safety in your team(s).

Encourage the team(s) to suggest ideas for improvement.

Continue to measure and improve.

📖 Reading

The Fearless Organization: Creating Psychological Safety in the Workplace for Learning, Innovation, and Growth by Amy Edmondson

Psychological Safety: The Key to Happy, High-Performing People and Teams by Dan Radecki and Leonie Hull

🌐 Links

Google re:Work guide: Understanding team effectiveness:
https://rework.withgoogle.com/guides/understanding-team-effectiveness/steps/introduction/

Building a psychologically safe workplace: by Amy Edmondson TEDxHGSE -
https://www.youtube.com/watch?v=LhoLuui9gX8&feature=youtu.be

People Not Tech: Psychological Safety Works
https://www.psychologicalsafety.works/

The Connector

Superpower: Connection

A resilient team is one in which employees have a shared sense of purpose and connectedness.

The Connector creates cultural experiences and means of engagement that allow for better collaboration.

The Connector encourages cross-functional collaboration to draw on the diverse set of skills and capabilities within an organization.

They provide cross-functional teams with a shared purpose and autonomy to solve problems, seize opportunities, experiment, innovate and make decisions within provided parameters.

During times of constant change, employees will face setbacks, challenges and high demands. This means that, as a leader, you need to invest in building networks and connecting teams with each other and other teams.

Leaders have to provide team cohesion through social activities, group training, celebration of individual and team achievements, regular informal team get-togethers and by creating a culture of mutual trust and respect. Leaders encourage employees to reach out to each other for support and maintenance of resilience.

You need to create environments where team members can share openly and fairly, and where they demonstrate empathy for others in the process.

By creating coalitions of networks, you can connect diversity of thinking, and ideas and solutions that lead to positive change and innovation. You can increase the speed at which problems and opportunities are addressed, and you can leverage the pool of knowledge, skills, expertise and experience across team disciplines, and industry and geographical boundaries.

In their words

Jason's story

As a leader in the property division, I had always been fascinated with the story of Steve Jobs and the building design at Pixar.

In 1986, Steve Jobs bought the small computer manufacturer Pixar.

In 2000, he relocated the company to an abandoned canning factory. The original plan was for three buildings with separate accommodation for computer scientists, animators and the Pixar executive. Jobs scrapped the plan and replaced it with a plan that had one building with an atrium at its center.

The purpose was to put the most important function at the center of the building—the interaction of employees. The atrium was a large open space where people could talk to each other. Jobs made sure this happened by placing the mailboxes, meeting rooms, cafeteria, coffee bar and gift shop in the center of the building.

When ABC Corporation head office needed to find new premises, due to growth, I worked with the design team and senior executives to come up with a similar plan.

The Pixar story resonated, and our new head office became one large building with a central area that housed the mailboxes, café, social areas, and coffee machines etc.

The results were amazing. Acting on the Connector superpower helped create collaboration across teams who had never interacted before. Our employee engagement went through the roof and levels of innovation soared. The central space might look like a waste of space, but as Steve Jobs knew, when people run into each other and make eye contact, things happen.

Actions

1. **Celebrate wins:** It is easy to get caught up in the speed of change without stopping to acknowledge successes and take time out to celebrate.
2. **Celebrate setbacks:** Setbacks should be seen as a learning experience and be celebrated along with the successes. Each setback is a step closer to success.
3. **Show gratitude:** Take time out to thank employees for their contribution. Be clear about what you are thanking them for. Do it publicly so others can share in the recognition.

4. **Reward:** Reward employees for their contribution and for going the extra mile. It doesn't have to be an expensive activity: a couple of movie tickets or retail vouchers say a big thank-you.

5. **Collaboration:** Emphasize the importance of collaboration within the team and outside the team. Encourage employees to reach out and collaborate across functions. Approach peers to engage in cross-functional collaboration on a particular project or change. Ensure there is a shared sense of purpose and goal.

6. **Team building:** There is an array of effective team building activities that can be leveraged to bring employees and teams together and establish a sense of cohesion and camaraderie.

7. **Time-out:** Provide a space for employees to take time out, decompress or socialize with each other. Use it yourself.

Reading

The Collaborative Organization: A Strategic Guide to Solving Your Internal Business Challenges Using Emerging Social and Collaborative Tools by Jacob Morgan

Extreme Teams: Why Pixar, Netflix, Airbnb, and Other Cutting-Edge Companies Succeed Where Most Fail by Robert Bruce Shaw

Links

The 12 Habits of highly collaborative organizations by Jacob Morgan - https://www.youtube.com/watch?v=dDe-iXDXqUA

The Five Stages of Emergent Collaboration (AIIM Conference 2012) by Jacob Morgan - https://www.youtube.com/watch?v=VwELvTy1z0w

The Reinforcer

Superpower: Reinforcement

The Reinforcer reinforces desired behaviors. Positive reinforcement builds resilience.

Much has been written about reinforcement theory. The basic tenet of reinforcement theory is that behavior is shaped and maintained by its consequences. Research has shown that employees who are positively reinforced, work together more efficiently and harmoniously and are more resilient in the process.[16]

Judith Komaki, in her book, *Leadership from an Operant Perspective,* built on this research. She revealed that effective leaders didn't give positive feedback more often than ineffective leaders but that the timing was different.

Effective leaders gave positive reinforcement while the employee was doing the job. The effective leader spends considerable time among their workforce in order to do this. Those spending most time in their offices are ineffective.

When you reinforce a behavior as it is being performed, you are clear about what you are reinforcing and the person receiving the reinforcement is also clear about the behavior that generated the positive feedback.

The longer the time between the behavior and the reinforcement, the less effective it is. This is exactly why annual performance reviews have little or no impact on behavior.

Individual and team resilience can also be supported when employees give positive reinforcement to each other. As a leader, you should encourage positive feedback at every opportunity.

Know your people

In order to provide effective positive reinforcement, you need to know your employees. What mix of reinforcements works best? Everyone is different and, therefore, will respond differently. What interests and motivates them? What is important to them?

It can take time to find this information, but it is simply acquired through conversation, listening and engagement.

Ask your staff what motivates them to get out of bed in the morning and come to work. Ask them what gives them the most satisfaction about their job. Dig deeper and find out what areas could be targeted as reinforcers.

You will need to use your effective communication and listening skills to gather the right information. Listen more than you talk. Don't interrupt. Encourage the other person to speak by showing interest in what they are saying. Maintain eye contact. Confirm that you have understood what they have said.

This engagement will tell you what to reinforce for each employee. Effective leaders possess a meaningful repertoire of reinforcement techniques, and they know how to use them.

Reinforcements could include (but are not limited to):

- Public recognition and praise
- Saying thank you
- Gift cards
- Concert or movie tickets
- Celebration breakfast / lunch / dinner
- Drinks after work
- Monetary rewards
- A pat on the back.

In their words

Jason's story

When I learned about the Reinforcer superpower, my initial reaction was "I have a large team. How am I going to find out what motivates each one of them so I can use the most effective positive reinforcement?"

I learned that I didn't have to find out that information overnight. It would take some time, and it did. I had many conversations, but I always kept a note of the motivations I uncovered.

I was always among my workforce, not being the 'office' sort of guy, so that part was not a problem. I could monitor what was happening, identify good behaviors and provide the positive recognition in a timely manner.

I also discovered that my relationship with my employees was paramount. Each time I had an interaction with an employee,

I could emphasize the link between their work and the overall objective of the team, which meant they had a sense of purpose.

Actions

One size does not fit all. You will have to customize your positive reinforcement to each individual.

Give positive reinforcement when it has been earned. Positive reinforcement is given when it is deserved.

Positive reinforcement is not an event, it is a process. Build positive reinforcement into work processes and relationships. Provide it on a regular and frequent basis so that people work at their best.

Mind the gap. Timing is important. Positive reinforcement should be given as soon as possible after the behavior you are reinforcing has taken place. The longer the gap, the less effective the reinforcement.

Overall, remember that it should be positive, immediate and certain.

Reading

Leadership From an Operant Perspective by Judith Komaki

Links

Positive Reinforcement in the Workplace (90+ Examples & Reward Ideas) -
https://positivepsychology.com/positive-reinforcement-workplace/

The Modeler

Superpower: Modeling

The Modeler models resilience.

As a leader, your employees are looking to you to model resilience. They want to see how you deal with the pressure of constant and uncertain change. They want to see you deal with setbacks, let-downs and failed attempts at success, and still bounce forward. They will take their cues from you, so it is imperative that they see you modeling resilient behavior.

The following are the behaviors that resilient leaders' model.

Change champions

These are champions of change. They don't resist it. They accept that constant change is the norm and they embrace it. They demonstrate that they are willing to change and provide the leadership for others to do the same.

They see the challenges of constant change as great opportunities. It is a chance to embrace the uncertainty and build on leadership strengths. You can show your integrity and ability to seize these opportunities even though they often don't present themselves as such at the time.

Quick to change direction

Resilient leaders are quick to make decisions and realize that there is no time for procrastination. They make a decision and if it is the wrong one, they are quick to change direction.

Failure is a learning opportunity

Resilient leaders don't see failure as a setback but as an opportunity to learn from it and move forward.

Rather than dwell on the negative, you can look at the positive and examine the lessons to be learned from the setback.

Signal intentions

Let everyone know what is going on. This requires effective communication. Communication that is clear and unambiguous. This allows others to understand changes and new directions, and observe effective communication in action.

Take risks

You have to demonstrate that you are prepared to take risks and try new things. The world of constant and uncertain change means we have to be ready to change with it. This means being bold and prepared to step outside of your comfort zone.

In their words

Prayash's story

When I talk to my team about resilience, I use two stories in particular.

One is The Stockdale Paradox written about by Jim Collins in his book Good to Great.

Admiral James Stockdale was held captive for eight years during the Vietnam War. He was repeatedly tortured by his captors and had no reason to believe he'd make it out alive.

He survived by accepting the reality of his situation and having healthy optimism. This contradictory way of thinking was the strength through which James survived.

Stockdale explained this idea as the following: "You must never confuse faith that you will prevail in the end — which you can never afford to lose — with the discipline to confront the most brutal facts of your current reality, whatever they might be."

The other is about Ernest Shackleton, the Antarctic explorer who departed with his ship Endeavour for the Antarctic on December 5, 1914. Shackleton and his crew were faced with one catastrophic event after another including being stranded on the ice, losing the ship, and avoiding starvation by eating the sled dogs.

Through all this, the crew were buoyed by a resilient Shackleton who kept a focus on the future and looked for solutions every step along the way. He accepted reality but maintained a healthy optimism. As a result, Shackleton and the crew survived.

I use the Modeling superpower and tell these stories to illustrate the resilient behaviors we should all strive to emulate.

Hopefully none of us will ever face situations like these. I see my role, as a resilient leader, to model optimism when faced with setbacks and provide my team with direction to move forward.

Actions

Model the behaviors as described in this chapter.

Be a change champion.

Be quick to change direction.

Embrace failure as a learning opportunity.

Clearly signal intentions.

Be prepared to take risks.

Reading

Lead By Example: 50 Ways Great Leaders Inspire Results by John Baldoni

Links

A Model of Mental Toughness by Ernest Shackleton
https://aqrinternational.co.uk/ernest-shackleton-a-model-of-mental-toughness

The Developer

Superpower: Development

The Developer creates a culture of learning. When change is constant and ever increasing in speed, leaders need to move from programs of training to a continuous learning and development model that repeatedly builds employees skills and provides a range of formal training options.

Traditional training used to be provided to employees at specific times, for example, onboarding, preparing them for new roles and enabling them to use new technology.

This was okay when the pace of change was relatively steady, but today it is relentless and as a result learning and development need to keep pace.

In addition to the traditional online and offline training courses, we need to expand our thinking to include learning on the job, developing cross-functional projects, enabling employees to share their skills and develop new ones, broaden the knowledge of how the organization works, use algorithms to match employee skills with enterprise-wide opportunities, and instill a growth mindset across the entire workforce.

Audit and reskill

Leaders need to determine the skills available today and the skills that will be needed in the future, and perform the gap analysis.

Back in 2013, AT&T undertook a systematic audit of its quarter of a million employees to catalogue their current skills and compare them with skills that would be needed in 2020 as it transitioned from a hardware company to a software company requiring skills in cloud-based computing, coding, data science and other technical capabilities.

The program called Workforce 2020 (WF2020) was a $1 billion initiative to retrain its existing workforce in new skills for new jobs.

The decision to retrain was made due to the limited supply of technical talent and high demand for it, and the high cost of turnover. Retraining employees for new or more highly skilled roles, allowed the organization to retain valuable organization-specific knowledge. The organizational learning curve was reduced through retraining as opposed to hiring externally.

When the pace of change is outrunning the skills of employees, organizations don't have time to go out to market for replacement labor with new skills.

It has estimated that, to date, AT&T employees have taken nearly 3 million online courses to help them develop new skills in areas such as cloud computing, data science, agile project management, cybersecurity and application development.

Talent fluidity

Often, organizations are not aware of the talent they possess internally; therefore, they are unable to match it to evolving requirements.

To overcome this challenge, office furniture manufacturer, Steelcase, created an online platform called Loop.

In a nutshell, Loop allows employees to create a profile, work is posted, and a simple algorithm is used to match talent to opportunity. Once the work is complete, profiles are updated.

This has benefits for the organization and the employee. As new requirements occur, the organization can quickly locate existing employees who have indicated interest in new opportunities and who have the skills to meet them. Employees can gain experience and develop new capabilities in ways their existing jobs simply didn't allow. This is like having an internal gig economy.

Continuous learning and growth mindset

In 1988, Dutch business executive and business theorist, Arie de Gues wrote that,

"The ability to learn faster than your competitors may be the only sustainable competitive advantage."

Today, the role of the leader is to help employees continuously learn. This means providing them with the tools and technology they need for increased collaboration, learning on demand, and the ability to find what they need, when they need it and from a variety of sources.

Leaders need to instill a growth mindset into employees.

Growth mindset

Carol Dweck coined the term "growth mindset" in her 2006 book *Mindset: The New Psychology of Success.*

Her research revealed that individuals who believe their talents can be developed (through hard work, good strategies, and input from others) have a growth mindset. They tend to achieve more than those with a fixed mindset (those who believe their talents are innate gifts). This is because those with a growth mindset worry less about looking smart and they put more energy into learning.

Organizations with a growth mindset are extremely powerful as they are on a continuous journey of learning and development. People are inspired to grow. They feel empowered and committed. There is increased collaboration and innovation.

Leaders must encourage employees. This requires them to be empathetic and understand where the employee is on their journey. They need to help them have courage to put themselves outside of their comfort zone. Having a growth mindset means being prepared to fail but embracing that failure as a learning opportunity.

Leaders can promote a growth mindset organization by hiring from within. As already discussed, ensure you know the talent that already exists within the organization. Ensure you know the motivated employees, and then match them with new jobs and opportunities.

In their words

Jason's story

I have always been keen to learn and develop but I also know that sometimes I have my defeatist head on and the words "I can't" permeate my thoughts. If I were having those thoughts, how could I expect my team to step outside of its comfort zone and learn or do something different?

I found that these steps helped me. So I called on the Developer superpower and used them with my team too.

Acknowledge that you and others are not perfect. We all have imperfections. It is what makes us who we are.

Listen out for that negative talk. Watch out for the "I can't do it", "What if I fail?", "I could do it if I had the talent", "I am just not good enough." When you recognize it, you can do something about it.

Talk back to your fixed mindset with a growth mindset. This means saying "I am not sure how to go about it, but I can work it out", "The most successful people have had setbacks along the way." Walt Disney was turned down 300 times trying to get funding for Disneyland. "Talent and skills can be learnt." As Michael Jordon said: "I've failed over and over and over again in my life. And that is why I succeed."

Have courage. Know that when you step outside your comfort zone, your comfort zone gets bigger. Reframe something you see as a challenge as an opportunity for growth.

Take small steps and don't try and eat the elephant in one go.

Reward yourself and your team along the way.

Develop a sense of purpose across the team.

These steps increased the appetite for learning and development across the entire team. Their motivation and desire for growth was amazing.

Actions

Encourage an audit of organizational skills and capabilities.

Audit your own team's skills and capabilities.

Work with the team, your colleagues and peers to determine the skills required by the end of the next ten years.

Identify the gap and determine actions to bridge the gap.

Action learning and development programs to provide employees with the new skills required for the roles of the future.

Encourage continual learning and development.

Get employees to set learning and development goals and objectives.

Discuss the progress toward the goals on a regular basis.

Hire new roles from within where possible.

Instill a growth mindset in your employees.

Reading

Mindset: The New Psychology Of Success by Carol Dweck

Links

Developing a Growth Mindset with Carol Dweck https://www.youtube.com/watch?v=hiiEeMN7vbQ

The Cultivator

Superpower: Cultivation

The Cultivator creates the environment for innovation.

Organizations that cannot innovate to stay ahead of the game will cease to exist.

Employees who do not feel safe to contribute through creativity, experimentation and innovation will have low resilience. Therefore, as a leader, you need to cultivate an environment in which innovation thrives.

Psychological safety

Psychological safety is key to innovation. An environment in which everyone feels safe to try new things, however crazy they may seem, is imperative. Everyone should feel free and safe to challenge the status quo and suggest potentially better ways of doing business.

Every idea should be heard and given space to be considered. It is easy to tear down ideas, but the best people bring bricks to help build something. See The Caretaker.

Encourage out-of-the-box thinking

Encourage people to challenge the status quo and think differently.

The Apple 'Think Different' campaign video transcript (1997) sums up the thinking that leaders need to encourage:

"Here's to the crazy ones. The rebels, the troublemakers, those who see things differently. While some may see them as the crazy ones, we see genius. Because the people who are crazy enough, to think they can change the world, are the ones who do."

Create an environment of imagination, exploration, and where people are free to ask "what if?"

Don't let the naysayers spoil the party.

Give people the time to think in this way.

Experimentation

Experimentation leads to innovation.

Leaders have to encourage experimentation. This means allowing people to try new things and to also get them wrong.

A "right first time" attitude will kill innovation. Experimentation is about making mistakes and learning from them. As Thomas Edison said, "I have not failed. I've just found 10,000 ways that don't work."

Reward and recognition

Recognize and reward those who are pushing the envelope and trying new things.

Recognition can be a verbal acknowledgment. Reward can be a couple of movie tickets or retail vouchers.

Innovation and experimentation should be honored.

Allow and celebrate setbacks

Setbacks are part and parcel of innovation. Every setback is a step nearer to success, so they should be celebrated as a learning opportunity. Analyze what went wrong and how to make it better.

Autonomy

Leaders have to provide autonomy for employees to innovate in their own way. Micromanagement is another killer of innovation.

See The Autonomizer.

Risk

Waiting until you have all the facts and data will not lead to innovation. Dee Hock, founder and former CEO of VISA said:

Making good judgements and acting wisely when one has complete data, facts and information is not leadership. It's not even management. It's bookkeeping. Leadership is the ability to make wise decisions, and act responsibly upon them, when one has little more than a clear sense of direction, proper values, and some understanding of the forces driving change. It requires true leadership. It requires those who can go before and show the way. It requires educing the inherent integrity and virtue that lies within everyone waiting to be aroused and brought into play."[17]

There has to be an element of acceptable risk in order to enable innovation.

Hiring

When hiring, leaders should seek out the innovators. These are the people who are intellectually curious. If they are asking questions about the organization and probing deeper than the information available on the company website, it is likely that their curiosity will continue once they have been hired.

Ask potential candidates to give examples of when they have experimented and come up with innovative ideas.

Everyone's business

Innovation is everyone's business. Leaders need to make innovation an integral part of every employee's job. Innovation does not happen behind a closed door with an Innovation Lab sticker on it.

Innovation often happens with the people working closest to the opportunity. The retail worker, the call center operative, the brick layer, the train driver etc. These are the people who, when encouraged to think creatively, will come up with innovative ideas for improvement.

In their words

Jason's story

My team had always felt safe to challenge decisions and the status quo. I had made sure that constructive conflict was welcome and there was psychological safety across the team. What I did notice, however, was that there was more problem identification than solution provision. We discussed this at a team meeting, and it became apparent that the team felt the provision of solutions was someone else's business.

It wasn't that the team wasn't prepared to be creative and come up with innovative ideas; it just wasn't seen as part of the team's job. That thinking did puzzle me, but it was what it was, and I needed to change the situation. I called on the Cultivator superpower.

As a team, we discussed what innovation looked like and I encouraged the team to reach out across functions to create teams for innovation.

I ensured that there was sufficient time to undertake innovation in conjunction with current jobs. Within weeks, we had some amazing ideas on the table. We had drones augmenting physical building inspections, automation of maintenance requests, people counters to drive automated changes in air conditioning settings, and building design using virtual and augmented reality.

Actions

As a team, define what innovation means.

Ensure everyone knows that innovation is everyone's business.

Create a safe environment for innovation—psychological safety— and take the quiz in The Caretaker.

Create teams of diverse thinking.

Provide collaboration tools.

Celebrate setbacks as learning opportunities.

Reward and recognize innovation.

Celebrate success.

Implement the successes.

Reflect on lessons learned and areas for improvement.

📖 Reading

How to Use Innovation and Creativity in the Workplace by Patrick Collister

The Fearless Organization by Amy Edmondson

Building a Culture of Innovation: A Practical Framework for Placing Innovation at the Core of Your Business by Cris Beswick, Derek Bishop and Jo Geraghty

🌐 Links

Internal Model of Reality by Dee Hock http://www.deewhock.com/essays/internal-model-of-reality

People Not Tech: Psychological Safety Works https://www.psychologicalsafety.works/

The Removalist

Superpower: Removal

The Removalist works to remove the stigma of mental health in the workplace.

Stigma can be one of the greatest barriers to psychological health and safety in the workplace; therefore, it can have a direct impact on employee resilience.

Often, employees who experience some form of mental health issue such as anxiety, stress or depression are reluctant to reach out for help due to a fear that their situation will be viewed in a manner that is detrimental to their character. They fear they will be seen as lazy, irresponsible, weak or dangerous.

We need to eliminate the stigma so that employees experiencing mental health issues can reach out sooner, access resources to assist and return to well-being. Generally, less than 1 in 3 employees struggling with a mental health condition seek help.

Removing the stigma not only helps employees already suffering a mental health condition but it also encourages other employees to talk about the subject. When there is no stigma, employees are encouraged and supported to seek help; they are more likely to know what resources are available to them to enable earlier recovery.

Be educated and informed

As a leader, you need to know the facts. You need to understand what mental health is and what it is not. Seek out training and resources to inform you. Find out if an employee assistance program (EAP) exists in your organization, and if so, what it can do to assist.

Language

Words and language can create a stigma around mental health and reinforce unfounded myths. We need to see a whole person whose mental condition does not define who they are.

Don't use language that denotes lack of quality of life for someone with a mental illness such as "she suffers from severe anxiety" or "he is struggling with depression."

The language used should not be emotional. Say it simply: "Mary has OCD" or "John has severe anxiety."

Speak up

If you hear someone talking derogatively about a person or their mental health, you need to speak up and challenge them.

Do not allow others to ostracize those with a mental illness by using terms in the wrong context such as "I am so OCD about tidying my locker" or "I think I will have an anxiety attack if that clock doesn't strike 5 soon."

Lead by example using the language outlined earlier.

If you think someone may have a mental illness, do not be afraid to reach out and have a conversation. See The Identifier.

Team culture

Foster a team culture that encourages open and honest communication and is able to discuss concerns such as stress, anxiety, depression, fatigue etc. without fear of any negative repercussion or of being judged.

Silence can be a killer.

Encourage the team to engage with stress management techniques such as relaxation, exercise, establishment of boundaries and taking time out to recharge.

Share it

Other people openly sharing their stories and experiences around mental health can be extremely powerful.

Invite speakers to talk to your team or the organization about how they overcame their mental health challenges.

If there are people within the organization who have had mental health issues, which they have overcome, ask if they would be prepared to share their story with others.

In their words

Sahar's story

Working in a call center can be an extremely stressful job at times. Generally, people are calling because they want something, or they have an issue. They don't call to check you are having a good day.

This organization is awesome in that it has a great employee assistance program, mental health education online, and mental health first aid officers on every site.

Despite these resources, I noted one of my employees seemed to be struggling and I reached out to him. Our discussion eventually revealed that he was extremely anxious and depressed as he didn't feel he was performing at his best.

He hadn't wanted to talk about it as he felt that it would be seen as if he couldn't do his job and he would be fired as a result.

I assured him that this would not happen, and we explored how and where he could get help. I provided ongoing support for him.

I realized that despite the resources available for people with a mental health issue, there was still a stigma associated with the condition and, therefore, the resources were not being utilized.

My action was to create a team culture in which we educated ourselves about mental health and talked openly and honestly about it. We challenged any myths or misconceptions that we came across.

It was a recurring item on our meeting agendas. Over the coming months, more staff reached out for help without being prompted. This doesn't relieve me from seeking ways in which to remove conditions that lead to mental health issues in the workplace, but it does reassure me that people feel able to ask for help. The Removalist superpower helped to do this.

Actions

Educate yourself.

See the whole person and do not allow their mental health condition to define who they are.

Encourage others to do the same.

Use the right language.

Challenge the misconceptions and inappropriate behavior of others.

Talk openly and honestly about mental illness.

Reach out and offer support.

Reading

Mental Health in the Workplace: Strategies and Tools to Optimize Outcomes by Michelle B. Riba, Sagar V. Parikh, John F. Greden

Links

Sane Australia -
https://www.sane.org/spotlight-on/workplace-mental-health

Heads up -
https://www.headsup.org.au/healthy-workplaces/what-is-a-mentally-workplace

People Not Tech: Psychological Safety Works
https://www.psychologicalsafety.works/

The Includer

Superpower: Inclusivity

The Includer builds a resilient team by fostering and modeling trust and inclusivity.

The Includer embraces the idea that an inclusive workplace is one in which injury, mental illness or disability do not present obstacles to a fulfilling life in work.

The Includer builds inclusivity through the creation of diverse teams. Diversity is not just diversity of age, cultural background, physical ability, race, religion, sex and sexual orientation—it also means diversity of thinking.

Including a diversity of people and thinking brings a broader knowledge base, a variety of perspectives, different cognitive mindsets and creativity.

Diversity brings variety that reduces errors and increases problem solving capability. If everyone in a team thinks the same way, errors may not be foreseen and problems will be unresolved. This is the result of groupthink.

Imagine that within your team you had a millennial who recently completed a Business of Digital Media university degree and someone who had been with the organization for over 30 years. This would mean your team had a broad knowledge base to enhance resilience.

The more perspectives a team has, the more discussion takes place around how problems can be overcome or opportunities seized. This results in more critical and differentiated assessments of situations.

Teams that include a range of voices and perspectives are better able to innovate, take risks, solve problems creatively, bounce back from failures and turn challenges into opportunities.

In their words

Prayash's story

When I commenced in ABC Corporation as the leader of the marketing team, I found that the team was a mirror image of the previous leader. The team consisted of the same age group, gender and mindset. It was clear that the previous leader had succumbed to what is a natural human tendency—to surround yourself with people just like you.

I knew that overcoming groupthink would be a challenge, so I put in place a plan to bring more diversity into the team. I did this using the Includer superpower.

When natural attrition occurred, I replaced that team member with someone very different from the others; I wanted to create more diversity.

I invited people from different functions, and of different tenure, ages and viewpoints to attend our team meetings and contribute to our planning for marketing initiatives.

At first, the team found it difficult to embrace the new contributions, so it took careful and considered interventions to bring cohesion to the extended team.

It resulted in ideas and approaches to our marketing challenges that would never have arisen before. By looking at the results, the team could see the benefits of including diversity of thinking. It became our way of working.

Actions

Create teams that are inclusive of diversity.

Hire for diversity of thinking.

Invite input from the youngest or newest employees.

Invite input from employees with the longest tenure.

Seek input from those closest to the action.

Build a team culture of open and honest communication, trust and mutual respect, constructive conflict and psychological safety.

Reading

Inclusion: Diversity, the New Workplace & the Will to Change by Jennifer Brown

🌐 Links

The role of diversity in organizational resilience: a theoretical framework -
https://link.springer.com/article/10.1007/s40685-019-0084-8

The Nurturer

Superpower: Nurture

The Nurturer builds a culture of trust and respect. When there is trust and respect, employees are connected. They feel safe to express their feelings knowing that there will be respect and their voice will be heard and valued. They trust you, as their leader, to be true to your commitments. It also reinforces that you trust *them* to do the right thing.

This results in resilience.

Leaders have to listen to their employees and seek their feedback on a regular basis. Everyone should feel comfortable sharing with you and their peers.

Provide education on effective communication, listening techniques and how to lead with empathy.

As a leader, you have to demonstrate that you care. You have to be accountable for any commitments you have made. When employees give you feedback, you need to show that you have heard them. If you cannot act on their feedback, tell them why that is the case.

The Nurturer encourages collaboration across the team and actively promotes team members to support each other. These behaviors are encouraged and reinforced. See The Reinforcer.

Every member of the team should be able to present as their authentic self. There is an environment of psychological safety built on trust and mutual respect. See The Caretaker.

In their words

Mayah's story

When I joined the company as the leader of the risk, audit and compliance team, there was little team cohesion. Team members were not very supportive of each other and they pretty much operated in isolation from each other unless work processes dictated otherwise.

After speaking with my team, colleagues and peers, I discovered that the previous leader had been a hands-on leader with a dictator-like manner. It was his way or the highway.

As a result, any trust and respect in the team was eradicated. Not only between the team and its leader, but between each other.

I engaged the Nurturer superpower and organized for an external consultancy and coaching organization to work with my team to reinstate the trust and respect that had been lost. Over a two-day, offsite workshop, we worked on communication and listening skills, learnt about each other, discussed what trust and respect looked like, and participated in activities to build trust and respect for each other.

This was a great success and team behaviors started to improve. New behaviors were recognized and reinforced on an ongoing basis and over time we had mutual trust and respect across the team.

Actions

Provide education in communication and listening.

Provide education about empathy.

Listen to each other.

Show your team that you care.

Support each other.

Encourage authenticity.

Be transparent.

Model a behavior of trust and respect.

Challenge behavior that does not promote trust and respect.

Recognize and reinforce behaviors of trust and respect.

Reading

Good to Great by Jim Collins

How to Get What You Want at Work: A Practical Guide for Improving Communication and Getting Results by John Gray

🌐 Links

Supersoul Sessions: The Anatomy of Trust by Brené Brown. https://brenebrown.com/videos/anatomy-trust-video/

The Promoter

Superpower: Promotion

The Promoter promotes self-care.

In our busy, always-on lives, we can often forget to look after ourselves. When we don't look after ourselves, we can become stressed, anxious, fatigued and burnt out.

Self-care is core to our resilience in a world of constant change. We need to look after ourselves and encourage others to do the same.

In addition to looking after their own well-being, leaders need to promote self-care for their employees. This includes leading by example.

Encourage employees to engage in activities that help them zone in on their senses. These need to be activities that they enjoy—not everyone likes yoga.

There is no one-size-fits-all but there are lots of sizes from which to choose. These include (but are not limited) to:

- Mindfulness: improve focus and concentration.
- Meditation: increase awareness and gain a healthy sense of perspective.
- Massage aids: relaxation and stress relief.
- Regular exercise: helps memory and thinking as well as looking after physical well-being.
- Detach from devices: can delay the release of melatonin; therefore, affecting sleep.
- Alone time: sparks creativity, builds mental strength, and increases empathy and productivity.
- Regular breaks: to refresh and recharge.

Leaders can provide time management, stress management, and resilience training.

Leaders can encourage employees to move by having "walking meetings" rather than sitting in an office.

Leaders need to afford employees the time and permission to look after themselves.

Wherever possible, leaders should ensure that the working environment is ergonomically sound and encourages movement, for example, sit / stand desks, distance to coffee machines, remote waste bins etc.

In their words

Jason's story

I was lucky in that I enjoyed meditation and keeping myself physically fit. I knew that this contributed to my mental and physical well-being. It wasn't until my manager and I started discussing ways to promote self-care and increase employee resilience that I thought about using the Promoter superpower to promote it across my team.

Rather than make suggestions that would result in eye rolls from the team, we had a meeting to discuss resilience, self-care and the options available to everyone.

We allocated activities across four categories: physical, professional, emotional / relationship and psychological / spiritual.

When we populated the categories, each member of the team created a self-care plan with one activity (or more) from each category. They shared their plans with the other team members; this established a sense of accountability.

They agreed to support each other in their endeavours and undertake some of their activities together, if that made sense.

After a month, I checked in on their progress and every member of the team indicated positive outcomes. These included feeling less stressed and anxious. We took our model and presented it to the management for consideration and rollout across the organization—which was done.

Actions

Help your employees to create a self-care plan across these areas as suggested by the Black Dog Institute.[18]

1. Physical: for example, exercising before work at lunch or after work, having a healthy diet, performing regular exercise.
2. Professional: for example, turning off work emails on the weekend, not eating lunch at a desk, going home on time, delegating where they can.
3. Emotional / Relationships: for example, making time for family or friends, going to the movies, recording three positive things about each day to show gratitude, having some "me" time.
4. Psychological / Spiritual: for example, keeping a journal, practising mindfulness, getting out into nature, learning to meditate.

Be a role model and demonstrate that you have a self-care plan that you follow.

Provide employees with support and encouragement.

Reading

Mental Health in the Workplace by Michelle B. Riba, Sagar V. Parikh and John F. Greden

Links

Spending 10 Minutes a Day on Mindfulness Subtly Changes the Way You React to Everything
https://hbr.org/2017/01/spending-10-minutes-a-day-on-mindfulness-subtly-changes-the-way-you-react-to-everything

Arianna Huffington's Thrive Program - https://www.linkedin.com/learning/instructors/arianna-huffington

Skill Share: Create a Perfect Morning Routine –

https://www.skillshare.com/classes/Create-a-Perfect-Morning-Routine/287216370

Why We All Need to Practice Emotional First Aid: Psychologist Dr. Guy Winch -
https://www.ted.com/talks/guy_winch_why_we_all_need_to_practice_emotional_first_aid?language=en#t-3801

The Accountant

Superpower: Accountability

Good leadership requires real accountability.

The Accountant is accountable, which means they take personal accountability for the choices they make and for their behaviors and actions.

The Accountant does not point the finger at others when things don't go to plan. They take ownership and act accordingly.

In a nutshell, the Accountant says, "the buck stops here."

Leaders with accountability assume ownership for the performance of their team. They are the captain at the helm and the only one who can be held accountable for the ship.

Accountable leaders seek opportunities for the organization to succeed and they champion those opportunities. They will question decisions that don't seem to be the best for organizational success.

When leaders demonstrate accountability, they are also modeling resilience.

Accountability means commitment, which is doing whatever it takes to get something done. It also means having staying power—this is resilience. It is about striving to reach the end-zone.

When leaders are accountable, they create trust within the team as they show commitment to delivering on their promises.

Leaders also need to build accountability within their teams. Each individual needs to be held accountable for their actions, so that the entire team can achieve its desired outcomes.

There will be circumstances, as a leader, when you want an individual to be accountable for outcomes such as in a crisis when you want them to take the lead. There will be other circumstances in which you want the team to be accountable such as needing collaboration for innovation.

Leadership accountability

Accountable leaders do the following four things:

1. They are honest. Accountable leaders are prepared to admit their own mistakes and say, "I stuffed up." They are honest about their strengths and weaknesses and work on personal improvement. They are authentic and prepared to show their vulnerability as they recognize that this is not a sign of weakness but a sign of courage.

2. They seek input. Accountable leaders don't think they need all the answers. In fact, they know they don't, so they seek input from team members, peers and colleagues. They are prepared to ask for help in overcoming a problem or seizing an opportunity.

3. They apologize. Accountable leaders readily say "I am sorry" when something for which they were accountable has gone wrong. They are prepared to make things right and commit to the actions needed. They don't focus on the mistake, they focus on successful outcomes.

4. They are decisive. Accountable leaders do not procrastinate in fear of making a wrong decision. They are decisive and will stand by their decisions regardless of outcome.

Team accountability

Leaders build accountability into their teams by doing the following:

1. They trust. You have to trust your team to do the right thing. If you micromanage, you are saying "I don't trust you."

2. They provide clarity. Make sure everyone is absolutely clear about your expectations.

3. They communicate. Keep the team focused and accountable through regular communication and feedback. Find out what additional support the team may need or obstacles that you can remove. Don't set the team up for failure.

4. They collaborate. Team members need to work together and they should hold each other accountable. There needs to be a regular team catch-up to check that everyone has done what they said they were going to do, and if not, what obstacles were in their way that can be removed.

5. They provide visibility. Make all progress visible. If things are not going to plan, don't immediately lay blame, instead, be curious. What happened? What could we have done differently? Give equal focus to the things that have gone well and the things that haven't. We often focus on the latter alone.

In their words

Mayah's story

When things went wrong in the team, individuals often pointed the finger and placed the blame anywhere but on themselves. There was no accountability. I needed the Accountant superpower. The first step I took was to make it clear that mistakes will be made and that there would be no adverse repercussion if the action leading to the mistake had been done with the right intent.

As a team, we discussed accountability and what that meant to each of us. We all signed a charter to be accountable for our actions and hold each other accountable for them.

At each team meeting, we would discuss the progress of various initiatives and the person accountable would provide the progress report with all the positive and negative things that had taken place.

There was no blame assigned. As a team, we discussed how to build on the positive and remediate the negative. Our blame culture was eradicated.

Actions

Lead by example and hold yourself accountable.

Discuss what accountable means.

Set clear expectations.

Trust and get out of the way.

Provide regular feedback. Discuss the things that went well and those that didn't without blame being assigned.

Get the team to keep track of everyone's commitments and to hold each other accountable.

Reading

Accountability: The Key to Driving a High-Performance Culture by Greg Bustin

Balanced Accountability: Leadership Secrets to Win Hearts and Maximize Performance by Hernani Alves

Links

A Powerful Pledge That Spreads Accountability in the Workplace | Garry Ridge l Freedom at Work Talks - https://www.youtube.com/watch?v=PQBszF6PIL4

The Director

Superpower: Direction

The Director provides clear direction for themselves and their employees. They provide clear direction but not at the expense of employee autonomy.

They provide clear direction without being prescriptive or micromanaging.

They enable resilience by providing clear direction, and when setbacks occur, they are able to get everyone back on track and working toward shared goals.

Everyone needs to know where they are going. If they don't, there is uncertainty and confusion. This lowers resilience.

As a leader, you set direction and create a shared sense of purpose where everyone is heading in the same direction to achieve shared goals.

The direction must be clear and unambiguous. It must be described in a simple language and be accompanied by a description of how everyone is going to move forward.

The direction a leader sets for a team or the entire organization is often referred to as the North Star.

In the past, mariners made their way through seas and oceans using celestial bodies such as the sun, moon and stars. The most popular and reliable was Polaris, also known as the North Star.

A North Star is the positive vision that a leader creates and shares. This points everyone in the right direction.

The North Star guides everyone toward achievement of vision and helps them move in the same direction.

Our world will continually change, just as the seas and weather conditions change, and we cannot control these changes. While these changes may alter our plans, we weather the storm and keep moving toward the North Star.

In his book, *The Power of Positive Leadership: How and Why Positive Leaders Transform Teams and Organizations and Change the World*, Jon Gordon writes about the telescope and microscope that leaders need on the journey to the North Star.

As a positive leader you will want to carry a telescope and a microscope with you on your journey. The telescope helps you and your team keep your eyes on your vision, North Star, and big picture. The microscope helps you zoom-focus on the things you must do in the short term to realize the vision in your telescope. If you have only a telescope, then you'll be thinking about your vision all the time and dreaming about the future but not taking the necessary steps to realize it. If you have only a microscope, then you'll be working hard every day but setbacks and challenges will likely frustrate and discourage you because you'll lose sight of the big picture.

The direction must include the following:

Vision

Explain why we are heading in this direction. Again, there should be absolute clarity and no room for misinterpretation. There has to be alignment with organizational vision, goals and direction.

Context

The reason for the direction must be believable. Employees (and other stakeholders) need context to understand why the priorities are important and the benefit it will bring to the organization and the individuals within it.

Expectations

The Director ensures the expectations of everyone are clearly articulated, and the outcomes and timeframes are clear and understood.

The why

When setting direction, it is important that everyone understands "why" they are heading in that direction.

It is often overlooked in preference of explaining the "what" and the "how." Employees need to know why, before you explain what it looks like and how we are going to achieve it. It's like telling me that we are going to London and we will get there by air and road. That tells me what and how, but it has no context as there is no why.

In their words

Sahar's story

My team didn't seem to have much of a sense of purpose, and it was hard for me to provide direction as I couldn't find an organizational direction with which to align.

The new CEO came on board at the same time as I became a team leader in the call center.

After a couple of months in the job, she did a road show around all of our geographical locations. She toured head office, our distribution centers and our retail stores.

Her key message was that the organization needed to change because the competition was fierce and was leveraging technology in ways that we had not even thought about.

While the organization embarked on a digital transformation, our direction was to work toward increasing customer satisfaction so we could keep our customer loyalty as we changed.

She ended her message with "This is our direction, I look to you to take us there."

She didn't tell us what needed to change or how we were going to do it. She just told us why.

It was so powerful. This was the Director superpower in full force. I worked with my team to determine how we could increase our customer loyalty through our interactions in the call center. We had a direction and sense of purpose.

Actions

Determine organizational vision and direction.

Create a team vision and direction aligned with the vision and direction of the organization.

Set the North Star.

Clearly communicate why that direction is needed.

Use your telescope and microscope.

Tell inspiring stories.

Provide clarity of expectations.

Allow employees autonomy to map their course.

Keep reinforcing the direction and the "why".

Reading

Start With Why: How Great Leaders Inspire Everyone to Take Action by Simon Sinek

Find Your Why: A Practical Guide for Discovering Purpose for You and Your Team by Simon Sinek, David Mead, Peter Docker

The Power of Positive Leadership: How and Why Positive Leaders Transform Teams and Organizations and Change the World by Jon Gordon

Links

Leadership With Direction by Shelley Flett https://shelleyflett.com/wp-content/uploads/2016/05/Leadership%20with%20Direction%20-%20White%20Paper-%20Final%20-.pdf

Simon Sinek TED Talk – How Great Leaders Inspire Action -

https://www.ted.com/talks/simon_sinek_how_great_leaders_inspire_action?language=en

The Reflector

Superpower: Reflection

The Reflector provides time for individual and team reflection.

After any challenge, change or event that was perceived as stressful, the Reflector makes time to reflect on:

- What went well?
- What didn't go so well?
- What did we learn?
- What could we do better?
- What were the negative experiences?
- What were the positive experiences?
- How can we increase our resilience?

Use this as a post-event briefing to improve resilience.

The Reflector encourages every member of the team to reflect on their recent experiences. Discussion about the challenge and how employees coped is encouraged.

This activity facilitates team members in supporting one another. The process can include action planning for the team.

As well as conducting this activity after a significant event, it can also be carried out after a series of low-impact events that may have left the team feeling depleted and fatigued by change.

These reflection sessions are often called "retrospectives."

In their words

Jason's story

There is so much power in reflection. I used to hold reflection sessions after a significant change but there was a lengthy gap between sessions.

I used the Reflector superpower to reflect on what the IT teams were doing in their adoption of more agile ways of working. We initiated fortnightly retrospectives.

We looked at anything that had happened over the last few weeks and reflected on the good, the bad and what we learned. Not every retrospective resulted in an action plan but if actions did arise, one of the team would take ownership and report back at the next retrospective.

It was a great vehicle for engagement, collaboration, team cohesion and continual improvement.

Actions

Consider your frequency. How often are you going to hold reflection sessions? It could be after every significant change or every few weeks. Ask the team for its preference.

At each reflection, ask:

- What went well?
- What didn't go so well?
- What did we learn?
- What could we do better?
- What were the negative experiences?
- What were the positive experiences?
- How can we increase our resilience?

Make an action plan and assign accountability for fulfillment of the actions. As the leader, all of the actions do not have to land on your desk.

Reading

Dare to Lead by Brene Brown

The Reflective Leader by Alan Smith

Links

Reflective leadership: Learning to Manage and Lead Human Organizations - Süleyman Davut Göker and Kıvanç Bozkuş. https://www.intechopen.com/books/contemporary-leadership-challenges/reflective-leadership-learning-to-manage-and-lead-human-organizations

The Enquirer

Superpower: Enquiry

The Enquirer asks questions—a lot of questions.

Leaders have to stop telling people what to do. Effective leaders lead with questions.

When leaders have a conversation based on questions, employees feel valued, motivated and empowered. This helps build resilience in the team.

When you ask employees questions, you are telling them that you are interested in what they have to say. There are two types of questions. One looks at what has already happened and the other looks to the future.

Looking at what has already happened garners employee perspectives about the event(s). Questions include:

- "How did that make you feel?"
- "What challenges did you face?"
- "What would success have looked like?"

The forward-looking questions ask:

- "What could we do better?"
- "What should we stop doing?"
- "What should we do next?"
- "What ideas do you have?"

When leaders ask questions, they generate a conversation in which many voices can be heard. Those voices are curious, creative, innovated and engaged.

In their words

Mayah's Story

I naturally want to help people find answers, so I always ask questions but I interrupt with my solutions. As a result, there is little team motivation and ownership to drive change.

I had to focus on what it was I wanted to know and what questions I was going to ask, then allow the other person time to think and respond.

When I did this using the Enquirer superpower, there was a natural tendency for the person answering the question to take ownership of the outcome and take action accordingly.

For example, there was an audit that hadn't uncovered some discrepancies, which were found at a later time. It wasn't a devastating mistake but I needed to find out what had happened.

I asked the auditor, "What could we have done differently?" and allowed them to think and engage in the conversation. The auditor noted that the checklist they had been following had not noted the need to access certain documents and, therefore, they had been overlooked. Without a prompt, the auditor took an action to update the checklist immediately.

Actions

Ask one question at a time.

Brevity is king.

Listen to the answers. Really listen.

Ask authentic questions to which you want an answer. Don't disguise trying to lead a conversation with questioning—people will see through it.

Keep questioning and probing.

Ask follow-up questions.

Allow employees time to answer. Give them time to think. Don't prompt and fill the silence. Let the conversation run naturally.

Acknowledge what they are saying and show you are listening.

Reading

Conversational Intelligence: How Great Leaders Build Trust and Get Extraordinary Results by Judith E. Glaser

Good Leaders Ask Great Questions: Your Foundation for Successful Leadership by John C. Maxwell

🌐 Links

Good Leaders Ask Great Questions by John Maxwell
https://www.youtube.com/watch?v=cRtu-NKQAKE

The Restructurer

Superpower: Restructuring

The Restructurer uses cognitive restructuring to challenge negative and reactive thinking.

What we say and how we say it can shape how we think. What we think can increase the intensity of our emotions and the way in which we perceive difficult situations. Therefore, the use of negative language can create negative emotions, which will result in low resilience.

Leaders and the individuals in their teams can use cognitive restructuring to change the way they think about situations.

Leaders should challenge negative language such as:

- "I can't do it."
- "It isn't even worth trying."
- "I am stressed with the uncertainty of it all."

- "I will just avoid challenges as it is easier than having to face them."

These are all negative predictions and leaders should pay attention when they happen. When employees are thinking in this way, it is hard for them to see any positive outcomes.

As a leader you can do the following:

- Calm the situation. Take your employee to a quiet place like an unused room or an outside space and get them to breathe deeply.
- Ask your employee about how they are feeling and what has triggered that feeling. It is important to understand the triggers and the emotions that resulted. When we know the triggers, we can manage them. If your employee is making unfounded assumptions about a current situation or future situation, dispute them in a positive and considered manner.

Leaders need to be mindful that negative language like "I can't do that" can stem from low self-esteem and lack of confidence. Therefore, it is important to determine what is underpinning the negative language.

Leaders need to help the employee reframe the situation and look at it from a positive angle. They need to provide a new perspective that will keep employees motivated and inspired.

In their words

Jason's story

Three years ago, I was working on obtaining additional retail space in a large shopping mall that had just been constructed. I didn't get the contract. The space was given to one of our competitors. My immediate feeling was that I was worthless and not capable of doing my job.

With the help of my manager and the Restructurer superpower, we did some cognitive restructuring / reframing.

The conversation with myself went more like this as a result:

I didn't get the contract. It is obvious now that it was not meant to be and that the space would have been the wrong image for ABC Corporation. I have better insight now as to the sort of space we should pursue in support of our brand and image. Now I can shortlist the shopping center companies and locations that are a better fit and start a conversation with them.

Actions

Encourage and work with your employees to:

1. Pause. Take a breath and ask what just happened.
2. Identify the triggers.
3. Ask what they were thinking immediately after the trigger.
4. Ask what they were feeling.
5. Let them rate their emotional response on a scale from 1–10 with 10 being the most intense.
6. Reframe. Ask if they can look at what happened from a different perspective. Is there a more realistic and / or positive way to view the trigger?
7. Ask how they are feeling after the exercise. How would they rate their emotions on a scale from 1–10?

Encourage your employees to keep practising these steps.

Reading

Mind Over Mood: Change How You Feel by Changing How You Think by Dennis Greenberger and Christine A. Padesky

🌐 Links

Cognitive Reframing - How Do You Talk To Yourself?
https://www.youtube.com/watch?v=kFYw-GWiRpc

The Protector

Superpower: Protection

The Protector protects the team by making sure it has the capabilities and resources to be resilient.

The Protector's language and behaviors say, "I care about you and I value your contribution."

Leaders who protect their employees, support and stand up for them. They make sure they have everything they need to get the job done. They are not left to fend for themselves and flounder.

Protected employees are developed and coached to be the best they can be.

Leaders must protect their employees, wherever possible, from anything that might lower their resilience. This includes unnecessary distractions, poor prioritization of work, overload of work, unclear goals and outcomes, and unconsidered demands from other parts of the organization.

Leaders protect by encouraging employee personal well-being and modeling resilient behaviors. They provide autonomy and self-direction, and they are consistent, fair, honest and transparent. They provide opportunities for employees to recharge.

In their words

Jason's story

My first job with ABC was in one of the retail stores. I was assigned to the men's shoe department. I had only been there two weeks and I was serving a customer when one of the managers from the men's clothing department approached me and insisted that I find a pair of shoes to match a brown suit that he was holding.

I tried to explain that I would help him after I had finished serving my current customer and that I was on my own.

The manager walked off in a temper and returned when my customer had left. He was aggressive, kept swearing at me and telling me that I was lazy and that he had lost a sale due to my unwillingness to help.

Being new, I just stood there and accepted it. Being fearful of further harassment, I wrote an email to my leader to inform her that she might get a complaint about me and I outlined what had happened.

The next day, she took me aside and asked me to describe what had happened again. She said to me, "Jason, no-one deserves to be spoken to like that. Next time that happens, you just say that you will have to revert to your manager. I have your back."

Although I sort of knew that is what I should have done, I had just frozen in the moment. Her reassurance really helped me.

She told me she would take care of it. A couple of hours later, the manager who had harassed me, came to me, and apologized for his behavior. He told me that there had been mitigating circumstances but that did not justify his behavior and he hoped that I would forgive him.

I knew, at this point, that my manager not only said she had my back but she actually did have it. She truly had the Protector superpower.

Actions

Make sure everyone knows you are there to protect them. Let them know you have their back. Look them in the eye and mean it. Be absolutely sincere.

Discuss with the team that protection means providing a safe workplace, capabilities and resources for resilience, clarity of expected outcomes, open and honest conversations, and care for their well-being.

Keep checking in and observe what is going on. Ask, "Are you ok?" "How are things going?" "How can I help?"

Most importantly, take action. You have to keep your promise to protect your staff.

Reading

Leaders Eat Last: Why Some Teams Pull Together and Others Don't by Simon Sinek

🌐 Links

Why good leaders make you feel safe by Simon Sinek TED 2014 - https://www.ted.com/talks/simon_sinek_why_good_leaders_make_you_feel_safe?language=en

Acknowledgments

My deep thanks go to:

Breed Barrett for her undying support, encouragement, contribution and patience.

Sylvie Blair at BookPOD for her ongoing help and guidance.

Jo Yardley at The Editing House for her attention to detail and excellence.

Peter Phan at Flimp Studios for the cover and illustrations and for bringing the Resiliator to life.

Working with Karen

You can engage Karen in the following ways:

Program Facilitator

- Unleash the Resiliator within – for leaders
- Unleash the Resiliator within – for individuals
- Change management coalition capability
- Change network enablement
- Adaptive leadership
- Adaptive leadership teams
- Leadership development optimized
- Need for speed – new tools for a new age
- Agile change management
- Leaders let go
- Change is everyone's business
- Creating a culture for innovation
- When everyone leads

Trainer

Training courses are available for all levels of your organization and are based on any of the programs.

Speaker

Keynote speaker for your next event based on any of the programs. Keynotes are tailored to your needs and those of your organization or audience.

Coach

Coaching for teams and individuals who need to evolve in line with the evolution of the business.

Coaching for change practitioners needing to revise their approach to align with the speed of change in the organization.

Coaching for leaders who need to become more effective and adaptive.

Mentor

Grow and learn through a mentoring relationship with Karen by sharing in her wisdom and experience.

Author

Contributing thought-provoking content for your next publication.

Connecting with Karen

Twitter: @karen_ferris

LinkedIn: https://www.linkedin.com/in/karenferris/

Facebook: https://www.facebook.com/karenferristhoughtleaderOCM/

Instagram: karenferrisdotcom

Endnotes

1 https://www.gallup.com/workplace/238079/state-global-workplace-2017.aspx

2 https://news.gallup.com/businessjournal/190445/negative-impact-disengaged-employees-germany.aspx

3 https://news.gallup.com/opinion/gallup/193490/unhappy-state-local-government-workers-cost-billions.aspx

4 https://www.talentforgrowth.com/engagement/disengaged-employees/

5 https://www.who.int/mental_health/in_the_workplace/en/

6 https://www.headsup.org.au/docs/default-source/resources/beyondblue_workplaceroi_finalreport_may-2014.pdf

7 https://www.who.int/mental_health/in_the_workplace/en/

8 https://www.victorianchamber.com.au/news-media/all/2019/11/workplace-manslaughter-laws-and-proposed-coverage

9 https://www.bbc.com/news/world-europe-50865211

10 https://www.paycor.com/about

11 https://www.google.com/about/

12 https://www.cisco.com/c/dam/en_us/training-events/employer_resources/pdfs/Workforce_2020_White_Paper.pdf

13 https://www.ruok.org.au/how-to-ask

14 https://www.apsc.gov.au/sites/default/files/working-together-mental-health-wellbeing-accessible.pdf

15 https://rework.withgoogle.com/guides/understanding-team-effectiveness/steps/identify-dynamics-of-effective-teams/

16 https://positivepsychology.com/positive-reinforcement-workplace/

17 http://www.deewhock.com/essays/internal-model-of-reality

18 https://www.blackdoginstitute.org.au/news/news-detail/2018/10/04/how-you-can-empower-your-team-with-self-care-planning

References

Collins, J. (2001). *Good to great*. Century.

Dweck, C. (2007). *Mindset: The New Psychology of Success*. New York: Ballantine Books.

Edmondson, A. (1999, June 1). Psychological safety and learning behavior in work teams. *Administrative Science Quarterly*. Retrieved from https://journals.sagepub.com/doi/abs/10.2307/2666999

Edmondson, A. (2018). *The Fearless Organization: Creating Psychological Safety in the Workplace for Learning, Innovation, and Growth*. Wiley.

Gordon, J. (2017). *The Power of Positive Leadership: How and Why Positive Leaders Transform Teams and Organizations and Change the World*. Wiley.

Komaki, J. (2015). *Leadership From an Operant Perspective (People and Organizations)*. Routledge.